Poetic Meditations

From the Throne

Jeri Darby

Poetic Meditations

From the
Throne

Jeri Darby

Stepping Stones
Soar into Your Destiny!

Ararity Press

First Printing 2019
Printed in the United States of America

ISBN 978-0-9979399-4-1

We ARE Sons & Daughters of The King of Kings! Own it!

The King's Daughter
Jeri Darby

The King's Daughter

There is none like you

My Beautiful Daughter.

You are in passionate pursuit of

My Living Water.

Before the watching world,

I will bless you Jeri.

Do not fret, doubt, faint or even grow weary.

I watch as you grow from glory to glory.

Proclaiming my Word,

Telling My Story.

Despise not the days of small beginnings.

In due season I shall unveil

Your happy ending.

Your Father, The King

Dedication

This book is dedicated to all my gifted Sisters and Brothers in Christ, whom I may never encounter in this life. Yet I pray that you will not allow satan to belittle your God-given talent. Instead, stir up, cultivate and release the gift of God within you to bless the families of the earth!

Table of Contents

Preface

Poetry is a beautiful expression in any language. It impacts the heart and mind with wisdom and insight while disbursing ah-hah moments. Most of these poetic eruptions were penned during a time that I sensed a supernatural flow of rhymes. Complete poetic expressions were released from my innermost being day after day and night after night.

At first, I embraced this newest experience during my late twenties. Grabbling for my pen and paper that I carried in my pocket, purse or laid on my pillow at night—I eagerly sought to capture *every* single word. This proved tedious and tiring. Poetry commanded my attention and often intruded on my activities during the day and at night my sleep was disrupted by rambling for my pen to scribble notes while half awake.

So—I had a conversation with God. "God I really appreciate the poems that you are giving me—but I could really use a break from the constant outpour of words." I explained how difficult it was to capture *everything* that he desired to share. Not my finest moment.

I later realize that I had grieved the Holy Spirit who was attempting to launch me into my purpose which is writing those words that I hear flowing from God's Throne. God, being a Gracious Father gave me a break—but nothing like I expected. He gave me a lo----ng break! The words dried up immediately and for the next ten years I experienced a severe word drought.

Words no longer flowed effortlessly. For years I could barely squeeze out a single poem! Though I can write poetry now it has never been as free flowing as it was during that season. I did not give my gift the appreciation and respect that it deserved. It became familiar and I took it for granted. God helped me to see that people were crying out to Him day and night for creativity. Lesson learned.

I began actively pursuing and praying for restoration of the poetry gift which was once so abundant in my life. God is faithful and the flow of words returned; but in different manners. Today they manifest in sermons, books, songs—and yes sometimes even poetry. I have a newfound appreciation and respect for words—especially those coming from God's throne. They are potent! And sent with purpose.

While writing this book I excavated poems—some I had forgotten that I ever wrote. What value is our writing gift if our words are never released to speak into the life of others?

If God has endowed you with the ability to utilize words in any creative fashion, submit your gift back to Him. Resist the temptation of allowing satan to pervert your God given gift. Allow God to use you to be a blessing to the families of the earth—this is His original intent for your life.

Introduction

A poetry book? Such thoughts flew in and out of my mind over the years; but I never gave them serious consideration. Then I crossed paths with a woman named Alberta Culpepper. She motivated me to plunge forward with this project and I started working on "Poetic Meditations from the Throne."

Alberta is an 86-year old woman who amidst a life-threatening illness determined to publish her book of poetry. I was honored to assist with the process of releasing her first book. Her determination was contagious. Once her book released—I thought, *"Why not poetry?"* My poetry book was completed a few weeks later.

My poetry has been stashed away and shared sporadically over the years. *Poetic Meditations from the Throne* are words that filled my spirit during quiet times of fellowship in God's presence. The poems in this book cover various life issues we face while riding the emotional roller coasters we find ourselves getting on and off throughout life. Poetry has a way of connecting with our deepest, traumas or our purest joy. It can cause our heart to smile or like a healing balm soothe our innermost pain. I pray that this book will impact you in such ways.

"It was
at that age,
that poetry came
in search of me."

Pablo Neruda

"Then
spake Jesus again
unto them, saying, I
am the light of the
world: he that followeth
me shall not walk in
darkness, but shall have
the light of life."

John 8:12 KJV

Son Light

I walk in the light of the Son

In my life, His will shall be done.

The thief comes to steal, kill and destroy,

Jesus brings Life, Peace

Love and

Joy.

Under God's shadow you can find rest,

Be assured, He knows what's best.

Ask-Seek-Knock

You shall receive,

If in your heart you can

Only believe.

I Am
The
Lord
That healeth thee.

Exodus 15:26 KJV

The Great Physician

I often wept with grief about
The tragedies of my past.
By the grace of God, I am whole
Festered wounds have healed at last.

What satan meant for evil
God used only for my good.
I never deemed this possible
Though God promised that He would.

Wounds penetrating deeply
Buried within my heart
Every time I thought they were healed
Such excruciating pain would start.

His healing light shone through me
My pain began to dissolve
I left His presence knowing
My concerns He would resolve.

He is a Great Physician
The miraculous He can do
He will not only heal your body
But your wounded emotions too.

And he said unto me,
My grace
is sufficient for thee:
for my strength is
made perfect

in

weakness.

2 Corinthians 12:9 KJV

`11

Breakthrough

If you're seeking for a breakthrough
Of God's spirit and His power.
If you need your strength renewed
And you need His blessings in this hour.

Then you must press against the fear,
Against the worry and the doubt.
Remember, God is here,
And He *will* bring you out.

Through all the tests and the trials
You may think your strength is small.
But if you continue to press,
God will see you through them all.

Just think about an unhatched chick
See it struggling through its shell.
It may think those walls are thick
For it has no way to tell-

That eggshells are thin
And shatters easily with a fall.
It is fighting with all it can
As it breaks outside those walls.

Barriers in our way
Whether fragile or hard as steel,
They come to pass, not to stay,
Just keep walking in God's will.

Since therefore
Christ has suffered for
us in the flesh,
arm yourselves likewise
with the same mind:
for he that has
suffered in the flesh
has ceased from sin;
1 Peter 4:1 KJV

Arm Yourself Likewise

Often people come to Jesus
Because they need relief
The problems of this world
Has caused them suffering and grief.

Accepting Christ into their hearts
Festered wounds began to heal
The brokenness of their soul
He restores and rebuilds.

Wouldn't it be nice
To right here end this chapter
With those famous last words
"They lived happily ever after."

You were thinking "My pain is over
My suffering is through!"
And begin to feel betrayed
When new trials came to you.

Let's take a moment to reflect
On the life of Jesus Christ
He was pure, He was holy
And He always walked upright.

He suffered greatly in this world
And quite unjustly so
I wonder how He felt inside?
You and I may never know.

He chose to love His persecutors
Though betrayed and falsely accused
Then for their iniquities
He was wounded, beaten and bruised.

Though legions of angels He commanded
He chose to suffer and die
Having a Heavenly Father
Willing to heed His faintest cry.

You want to be just like Him?
Are you willing to pay the price?
Abundant blessings awaits you
But there are some sacrifices.

One thing to remember
When facing worry and despair
Shut off the voice of satan
Don't let Him whisper in your ear.

He will say, "You're all alone
God has forsaken you and left
And you might as well give up
Rather than making another step."

He will tell you that, "God's the reason
For everything you're going through!"
Of all the things He tells you
None of them will be the truth.

The time is *NOW* to arm yourself

Put on the very mind of Christ
Let God get all the glory
For the suffering in your life.

He's not the cause of your suffering
He's the cure for your pain
While satan's plan and purpose
Is to drive you insane!

And they
shall be mine, saith the
LORD of hosts, in
that day when I make
up my jewels; and I
will spare them, as a
man spareth his own
son that serveth him.

Malachi 3:17 KJV

Precious Gems

"What is man that thou art mindful of him?"
In my mind I often wondered.
"To me, my child they are precious gems
Despite all their sins and blunders.
They are rubies, diamonds, emeralds and pearls
And I long to be their friend.
The most priceless jewels in all the world
For them I would die again.
Many of them never realize
The great value which they possess.
But they are my most treasured prize,
My work of art, my best!
While man looks on the outer appearance
I'm looking deep within.
My heart just overflows with joy
As I adore them again and again.
My most sincere and earnest desire
Is for them to know their true worth.
But this someone must inspire
Starting right from birth.
I need someone to tell them
Of a God whose love is true.
And for His lovely, precious gems
There is *NOTHING* that He wouldn't do."

Be sober,
be vigilant; because
your adversary
the devil,
as a roaring lion,
walketh about, seeking
whom he may
devour.

1 Peter 5:8 KJV

To the Innocent Man

Just being in the wrong place
At the wrong time
Can place you right smack in the middle
Of the scene of a crime.

You may be innocent
But that won't matter,
All your hopes and dreams
Have just been shattered.

Loved ones warned, saying
"You are on the wrong track!"
But you laughed at them
Time they turned their backs.

"It's all a big mistake!
You explain again and again
But no one's listening
Oh yeah, where's all your friends?

Now no one believes
A word you're saying is true
And all of the evidence
Points directly at you!

You used to go to church
Sometimes twice on Sunday
But forgot everything you heard
When you awoke on Monday.

You had a blast hanging out
In all the wrong places
Running all over town
With all the wrong faces.

Now you're praying to the Lord
To have mercy on you.
While sitting in prison
For a crime you didn't do.

Might as well make the best
Of this bad situation
While *The School of Hard Knocks*
Sponsor your education.

Despite everything else
You are still God's child
He loves you even though
You chose to run wild.

He loved you then
And He loves you now
He will work things out
Someway, somehow.

God has a way
Of turning things around
And when He's on your side
You can't stay down.

But here you must sit
Just God and you
The ball's in your court
What are you going to do?

*For
we walk
by
faith,
not by sight...*

2 Corinthians 5:7 KJV

Potential

Potential...You have plenty,
But how much is it worth?
It's been wilting away inside you!
Since the day of your birth.

With sentiments of love
It was instilled by God your Father,
It needed cultivation
But you never even bothered.

You have what it takes
To set your dreams in motion
The answer lies in you
There are no magic potions.

It's time to break free
From whatever has you bound,
Who's to say that what you have
Couldn't turn this world around?

A book? A Poem? Invention?
Just waiting to be expressed,
It may be through your work
That this nation will be blessed.

Your potential trapped inside
You must find a release
Or else with you it shall perish
On the day that you are deceased.

"Before
I formed
you in the womb I
knew you;
Before you were born
I sanctified you;
I ordained you a
prophet to the
nations."

Jerimiah 1:5 NKJV

He Knew

God is not amazed
By your achievements.
He's not confounded
By your problems.
He cannot be intimidated
By your anger.
He's not embarrassed
By your weaknesses
Your fears are not
Disappointing to Him.
No aspect of your being
Has caught Him off guard
Before creation
All that you are...
All that you were...
All that you'll ever become
He knew...

Rejoice
with them that do rejoice,
and
weep with them that weep.
Be of the same mind one
toward another.

Romans 12:15

Is it SAFE?

Is it safe...?
To share with you my grief and fears?
The pain I've stuffed inside throughout the years.
When I'm alone, my aching heart cries silent tears.
Is it safe...?

I get tired...
I really need to share my grief and pain.
Then I ask, what would I lose, what shall I gain?
Then at times, I feel just like I'm going insane.
I get tired...

People ask...
Aren't you glad, that you have the victory?
Now that you're saved, delivered and set free.
Although I smile, my heart is heavy as can be,
When people ask...

I love the Lord...
He is my strength, He is my source.
I worship Him, I lift my hands, I lift my voice
No matter what, He will always be my choice.
I love the Lord...

It would be nice...
To trust someone with all the things I'm going through?
To share my grief and celebrate my victories too!
To show concern when others were ever sad and feeling blue.
It would be nice...

But IS IT SAFE?

Be anxious for
nothing, but in
everything by prayer
and supplication,
with thanksgiving, let
your requests be made
known to God...

Philippians 4:6 KJV

Be Anxious for Nothing!

Trusting in the word of God
I don't always see my way.
Concerns with daily struggles of life
Can grow from day to day.

Comfort unfounded in earthly friends
Anxiety and worry increase.
Then I remember my Heavenly Father
Whose wonders never cease.

The mail carrier is faithful
They will always deliver my bills.
But I cast these cares upon the Lord.
For this is His perfect will.

My automobile needs repair
And my washer broke down too,
Thank God for His grace and peace,
Or else what would I do?

He has always been faithful
Throughout my entire life.
That's why I know I can trust Him
With difficulty and strife.

His Word says "be anxious for nothing"
But express gratitude in prayer
Make your request known unto Him
And be patient, He will be there

He that dwelleth in
the secret place
of
the most High
shall abide under the
shadow of the
Almighty.

The Secret Place

Lord I sit
Waiting, anticipating
In your Holy presence
Quiet, yielded, still
As I listen for your will...

Prayers of thanksgiving, petitions
Supplications, praise
Are erupting from deep within
Heavenward ascending before your throne
Saying yes, yes, yes...I desire to be your own...

For it is in your Awesome presence
That worries of today
Agonies of yesterday
Fears and doubts of tomorrow
Are all uprooted, cast down, plucked out
And your perfect peace is all about...

There is a secret place
Demons, devils, all the forces of hell and darkness
Seek to enter, while treading to and fro
Meanwhile praises to God I sing
While resting safely beneath His wings...

Behold,
I will do a
new thing; now it
shall spring forth;
shall ye not know it?
I will even make a
way in the
wilderness, and rivers in
the desert.

Isaiah 43:19 KJV

The Desert

You hid me in a desert place
And instructed me to seek your face.
At first I did not understand
Why this dry and thirsty land?

I thought my soul would fade away
But you renewed my strength from day to day.
I pleaded with you my soul to water
You said, "Fear not, I'm with you my daughter."

The arrogance, the pride, the strife
I must remove them from your life."
He said, "Don't try to reason why
You see, your flesh, it has to die.

Right now I know that things aren't clear
Remember I am always near.
Just walk by faith and not by sight
I will do the miraculous in your life.

Keep your spirit in tune to my voice
I AM your God! I AM your source!
I will bring you from this desert land
Where living waters shall flow again."

But Jesus said,
Suffer
little children,
and forbid them not,
to come unto me:
for of such
is the kingdom of
heaven.

Matthew 19:14

The Children

Take the children by the hand
We must help them understand

Our Savior's Plan...

With love, patience, and affection

Give them gentle firm correction

They need direction...

Teach them cautiousness—*not* fear

Tell them Jesus really cares

Help them hear...

You will
also declare a thing,
And it will be
established for you;
So light will shine on
your ways.

Job 22:28 NKJV

My Confession

I
Have strength!
Life
Has taught me

That I am strong.

In fact

I am stronger than
I
Think I am.

I am as strong as I

Need to be.

When I am Weak

I

Am Strong.

His strength is perfect

When my strength is Gone.

While

the earth remaineth, seedtime and harvest, and cold and heat, and summer and winter, and day and night shall not cease.

Genesis 8:22 KJV

The Harvest

When you sow

Unselfishly

With gladness of heart

With integrity of spirit

Then, the harvest must come.

When you wait...

With anticipation

In obedience

Patiently

Then, the harvest must come.

I

Can do all

Things

Through Christ

Who strengthens

Me.

Philippians 4:13 KJV

Equipped

I am capable of doing
What God ordains for me.
Although, sometimes I wonder,
"Lord, how can these things be?"
Feelings of self-hatred,
Insufficiency and lack,
Will not get me to my purpose,
They will only hold me back.

I refuse to continue
To be paralyzed by fear.
For such a time as this
Is the reason that I'm here!
I can feel Him pulling, tugging
In the depths of my soul.
Bringing forth what He inspired
For the world to behold.

I shall seize each moment
With joy and anticipation,
And praise Him as He teaches me
To excel in new situations.
I am well equipped
I have His Spirit and His Word.
His eye is on the sparrow,
But He loves me more than birds.

Put on
the whole armour
of God,
that ye may be able to
stand
against the
wiles of the devil.

Ephesians 6:11,12 KJV

War!

Warfare has been waged
And the thing that you will find,
It's not fought with knives and guns
But right within your mind.

Satan hunts for crevices
Where he can enter in,
Once he has gained access
Deceitfulness begins.

Sowing seeds of greed, lust,
Envy, jealousy and strife.
Once these seeds are rooted
They breed confusion in your life.

For protection wear God's armor
Gird up the loins of your mind.
Think on things that are pure, lovely,
Gentle, meek and kind.

Meditate on the Word of God,
Hide it within your heart,
A good work God has begun in you,
And He finishes what He starts.

You

are snared

by the words

of

your mouth;

You are taken by the

words of your mouth.

Proverbs 6:2 KJV

Hung

Have you ever wondered,
"Why can't I get ahead?"
Hopes, dreams and visions
All buried within you, dead.

Do you want to birth new vision?
Do you want to find new zeal?
Then I must tell you something
That's simple, true and real.

The tiny organ of your speech
Planted just beyond your lips
Directs the course of your life
As the helm guides a ship.

Good... Unjust... or Evil...
Words produce after their own kind.
That's why it pays to heed
What you allow to enter your mind.

My brother, my sister I beseech you,
Watch how your words are flung.
Or else you may be next
To be hung by the tongue...

`54

"*Father
of
the fatherless
and
protector of widows is
God in his holy
habitation."*

Psalm 68:5 KJV

He's Faithful

The Lord was with you in holy matrimony
You each pledged your eternal love
Entering a sacred union
Ordained from the heavens above.

He watched & blessed your marriage
Throughout tumultuous years
Through happiness, joy & laughter
Through tragedies, sorrows & tears.

Life's journey, you must continue
Though your partner is now deceased
God is a faithful provider
He'll give you grace, mercy & peace.

It is of the
LORD's mercies that
we are not consumed,
because his compassions
fail not.
They are new every
morning: great is thy
faithfulness.

Lamentations 3:22,23 KJ

Another Day!

Another day to walk in grace
To sing your praise and seek your face.
I pray that You restore my soul
Renew my strength and make me whole.

Help me to never be deceived
And in your word to always believe.
Use me Lord for Your glory
To speak Your word, to tell Your story.

Let me never be ashamed
To take a stand in Jesus name.
I pray that others plainly see,
The love of Christ which dwells in me.

I hope they too will make a choice
To listen for their Father's Voice.
And when this day is finally through
I pray I've won new souls for You...

And David inquired at the LORD, saying, Shall I pursue after this troop? shall I overtake them? And he answered him, Pursue: for thou shalt surely overtake them, and without fail recover all.

1 Samuel 30:8 KJV

Take it Back!

The kingdom of heaven suffereth violence,
And the violent take it by force."
When I chose to fight in God's army,
I certainly made the right choice.

Sometimes you must get angry
At your very situation,
Instead of wasting away inside
With agony and frustration.

A battle we are in
Whether we like it—or not.
We must have faith in Jesus
For He is ALL we got.

The enemy is here right now
To kill, steal, and destroy,
But a people who know their God
Can do great and mighty exploits!

On my enemy I shall trample
And keep him under my feet.
For God is my source
And I shall NEVER be defeated.

Satan has robbed, killed and stolen
From the people of God too long,
We have a prime directive
Coming straight from God's throne.

Saying, "**Arise** and **stand** in power,
Unify and *act*...
For *WHATEVER* the devil has stolen
It is time to *TAKE IT BACK!*

Call

unto me, and
I will answer thee,
and show thee great
and mighty things,
which thou knowest not.

Jeremiah 33:3

Solutions

My heart needed answers
To the confusion in my life
I sought to find solutions
To bring an end to all my strife.

But my solutions bought more problems
That I thought I could not bear.
The burdens drove me to my knees
Seeking God in prayer.

Yes—I wanted magic answers
To come and wipe my grief away.
The changes I desired
Began when I started to pray.

Now when my heart wants answers
Straight to God I go.
For I trust the right solutions
He will always know...

I will
go before thee,
and
make the
crooked places
straight...

Isaiah 45:2 KJV

The Crooked Places

Strange, new paths my feet discovered
Then I lost focus of my goals.
"Lord, make my crooked places straight!"
This urgent plea streamed from my soul.

Detouring down those crooked places
Bought only confusion pain and fear.
The highlights of this painful venture
Are marked by heartache, pain and tears.

"Lord! Make the crooked places straight!"
A simple cry bursting from my heart.
You used this plea to set in motion,
The brand-new life that I would start.

Suddenly— my whole life changed
Once my focus turned toward You.
I have experienced for myself,
Just what faith in God "can" do.

Be

ye angry,

and sin not:

let not the sun

go down upon your

wrath

Ephesians 4:26

Anger

It's *only* a
"F-E-E-L-I-N-G"
Acknowledge it...
Feel it...

Control it...

Express it...

Release it...

Then move on.

The thief
cometh
not, but for to steal,
and to kill,
and to destroy:
I am come that they
might have life, and
that they might have it
more abundantly.
John 10:10 KJV

Internal Nightmare

You may go through life wearing a smile
While others think, "Nothing ever gets you down."
But in your heart you are wearing a frown
Because your life is an internal nightmare.

If others could only see inside
All the agony and hurt you're struggling to hide.
You keep it hid because of your pride—
But your life is an internal nightmare.

Your focus, your dreams, motivation all gone
Day to day trying to carry on.
You're feeling weak, but acting strong
Because your life is an internal nightmare.

Your depression, oppression, confusion, and pain
Is enough to drive anyone insane!
Your mind is in a suicidal frame.
Wishing to end your internal nightmare.

Satan is pleased as he can be
For this was his plan and purpose you see.
Before you were born, he made a decree
To make your life an internal nightmare.

But there is one who sees, and He knows all
He's waiting for you to say "yes" to His call
He can help you to stand strong and tall
And bring an end to your internal nightmare.

Look up and live! There is hope today!
Jesus died, He's already made a way
He can bring to an end, *THIS VERY DAY!*
An end...to your internal nightmare...

I waited patiently
for the LORD;
and he inclined unto
me, and heard my cry.
He brought me up also
out of a horrible pit,
out of the miry clay,
and set my feet upon a
rock, and established
my goings.

Isaiah 40:1,2

Patience

I'm learning to take one day at a time
And be anxious for nothing,
when I don't have a dime.
Jesus encourages my heart each day,
I know He's there
Every step of the way.

My God, He provides my every need
My Heart's desires I shall receive.
He is my joy and my salvation He brings me through
In all situations.

I was once in a hurry to get ahead
Then I started to listen to what the Bible said.
"In your patience you possess your soul"
So I'm trusting God to achieve my goals.

As I lift my voice to the heavens and sing
Exciting new ventures each new day brings.
I'm excited for all that God is doing for me!
But I first had to learn to be patient you see.

The promises of God are as sure as gold
I pray to him standing strong and bold.
For the Father has good things lying in store
For those who will wait until He opens the door.

Death
and life
are in the power
of the tongue:
and they that love it
shall eat the fruit
thereof.

Proverbs 18:21 KJV

Life or Death?

Life or death is spoken
Each time you open your mouth
Hope is built or broken
By whatever you're talking about.

You speak your mind and leave
But your words will linger on
Having power to deceive
Or to make one become strong.

Living on in our minds
Are spoken words from long ago.
If they were considerate and kind
They probably caused you to grow.

But if those words were cruel and mean
Sent forth with anger and strife.
Their devastation may be seen
Throughout the rest of your life.

The results of your spoken words
Don't ever underestimate.
Will they be the cause or cure,
To create or devastate?

"Have I
not commanded you?
Be strong and
courageous. Do not be
afraid; do not be
discouraged, for the
LORD your God will
be with you wherever
you go."

Joshua 1:9 NIV

Calling the Courageous

Who would have ever thought
That we'd be living in a day like this?
Something has to be done
Far beyond a hope and a wish.

We hear daily reports of violence
And all sorts of hideous crimes
I think it has become quite evident
That we're living in perilous times.

Children have become murderers
It's not even safe in schools
There's truancy, insubordination
With no regard for authority or rules.

Certainly we can pray
And this I'll continue to do
But everyone must get involved
United God will take us through.

In your school, church, home or community
Are you willing to play a role?
This appeal isn't for cowards
It's a call for the courageous and bold.

Turn,
O backsliding
children, saith the
LORD; for I am
married unto you: and
I will take you one of
a city, and two of a
family, and I will
bring you to Zion:

Jerimiah 3:14 KJV

Thanksgiving of a Former Backslider

Jesus, My Lord what can I say?
How vividly I recall the day.
Sin had taken out its toil
And my soul was sunk in deep turmoil
Even though it was I who left
You restored to me your precious gift
You refused to leave me lost in sin,
And came to claim my life again,
Many long years I groped in darkness
My once tender heart was driven to hardness
In miry clay you found me lying
Knowing quite well my soul was dying
With your very own blood you cleansed me
thoroughly
While saying to me; "I love you surely,"
Within your courts I once more stand
Vowing to never leave again
I praise you Lord, My Savior, My King
And thanks again for EVERYTHING!

If
ye continue in
My Word,
then are ye
My disciples indeed.

John 8:31 KJV

Tenacity

I'm learning to be tenacious

By seeing things through until done.

You will never taste success

Without finishing that you begun.

Distractions come and go,

Even discouragement and defeat.

But every time you fall

You must get right back on your feet.

The race is not given to the swift

Nor the battle to the strong.

It goes to those who will conquer anything

To keep on keeping on!

Let everything that has breath praise the Lord...

Psalm 150:6 KJV

An Excellent Praise

A more excellent praise, my soul desires to give
Exuberating forth
Each moment that I live.

You are worthy of all praise, glory and honor too
My heart, my mind, my soul
My God I yield to You.

In the depths of my being, erupting deep within
Praises of thanksgiving
Heavenward ascend.

My sacrifice of praise, You lovingly accept
Your Spirit sweeps my soul
As cleansing tears are wept.

Such a meager thing, praises I pour forth
Kneeling in Your presence
Within Your inner courts.

Crouched at the throne, where reigns the King of
Kings
With pleasure He receives
The songs to Him I sing.

A more excellent praise, Dear Lord I yearn to render
A praise that is befitting...
Your Royalty and Splendor.

His divine
power hath given unto
us all things that
pertain unto life and
godliness, through the
knowledge of Him
that hath called us to
glory and virtue.

2 Peter 1:3 KJV

To Risk or Not?

There is a time to proceed with caution
And a time to jump in with both feet.
You will have your times of victory
And times of tears and defeat.

Life is full of change and challenge
Don't get stuck in a comfort zone.
To realize your fullest potential
You must be willing to keep moving on.

Others may try and fail
Or maybe they make no endeavor
To pursue their hopes and dreams
Although this is not very clever.

What's worth a risk for you?
Only you can decide.
And when to take a risk?
Let the Lord, *NOT* people be your guide.

`88

*I count
not myself to have
apprehended:
but this one thing I
do, forgetting those
things which are
behind,
and reaching forth unto
those things which are
before..."*

Philippians 3:13 NIV

~~SEIZE~~ The MOMENT!

I glimpse moments left behind me
Where I have failed to act
Some of those opportunities
May never again come back.

I used to feel remorseful
But I'm learning to look ahead
To things that are yet to come
Let bygones be dead!

God is moving by His spirit
His glory to reveal
To a holy vessel
Desiring to do His will.

To take to heights unknown
And pour out His power
To fill with His spirit
And use in this hour.

I shall seize this moment
To glorify His name
For those that trust in Jesus
Shall never be ashamed.

For God
hath not given
us the spirit of fear;
but of power,
and of love,
and of a sound mind.

2 Timothy 1:7

Letting Go...

Let go of human reasoning
For the earthly mind cannot conceive
The Abundance of God's resources
And His endless possibilities.

Mind boggling is the way of faith
Defying all wisdom of man.
It takes the foolish things and confounds the wise
Over and over and over again.

Through His word God has spoken
He's not a man that He should lie.
His word is what I will depend on
Until the day I lay down to die.

I have learned that this way of faith
Does not always make sense or seem clear
My experience thus far has taught me
To trust God and relinquish my fear.

"Eye
has not seen,
nor ear heard,
Nor have entered into
the heart of man
The things which God
has prepared for those
who love. Him."

I Corinthians 2:9 NKJV

Because of You

You called me with a holy call
I knelt before your throne.
You said that if for you I lived
That I would never walk alone.

Through visions, dreams and prophecy
You confirm your word in my life.
Through work, church, and family
You teach me to deal with strife.

Creative ideas daily unfold
While facing many uncertainties.
But I know beyond a shadow of doubt
That you placed these things in me.

You opened doors which no man can close
And others you have shut.
Studying your word it is clear to me
That I haven't seen anything yet.

Tiny, great, large or small
Whatever you want me to do,
My doubts, my fears, I release them all,
I'm here because of you.

`94

And they went forth,
and preached
Everywhere,

the Lord working

with them, and

confirming the word

with signs following

Mark 16:20 KJV

Miracle!

Lord I need a miracle!
Please put me in the frame of mind,

To receive a miracle from heaven

Of the supernatural kind.

It is time that I lie prostrate

Humbly before your throne

Entering the Holy of Holies

Where it's you and I alone.

Witnessing your great power

I have more faith than ever before.

But I want to get positioned

To receive all you have in store.

Fear not,
for I am with you;
Be not dismayed, for
I am your God. I
will strengthen you,
Yes, I will help you,
I will uphold you with
My righteous right
hand.

Isaiah 41:10 NKJV

Alone

Dear God,
I just want to say thanks.

Thank you for

Teaching me that I can be alone,

Without being lonely.

Thank you for

Showing me that

I could yet blossom,

Even during seasons

Of grief and solitude.

Thank you for

Teaching me that

When I'm with You,

I am never really alone.

And he said
unto him,
arise,
go thy way:
thy faith hath
made thee whole.

Luke 17:19 KJV

Wholeness

The single person
Is viewed with pity
By those looking
From without.

But it was through
My singleness
That I discovered,
What living was all about.

The single person
Is viewed as lonely
By married
Women and men.

But through
My singleness,
I have learned,
To be my own best friend.

The single person
Is often viewed
As a half,

Rather than whole.
But through my singleness
I discovered,
A completeness
Worth more than gold.

I

have fought the

good fight,

I have finished

the race,

I have

kept the faith.

2 Timonthy 4:7 NKJV

The Human Race

The human race, the human race, the human race...
(Song) "Whether yellow, black or white- they are
precious in..."
Wait a minute! How did the words race and color
Become synonymous?
This stretches far beyond the confines of my
intellect
Human race...someone heard these words
And begin allocating the world's population
By language, physical features, skin tones etc.
This unleashed segregation, hatred, discrimination...
Race, was never about color or separating people
Rather the term is a reminder
That as a people we are all eligible for a reward
A divine reward...
If we participate in and complete- the *race*
This competition is like none other on the planet
There is no first, second or third place.
Everyone who participates is potentially a winner!
The only stipulation is that the race be completed.
It doesn't matter how fast or slow your pace
Because this race is not given to the swift
It is not given to the strongest, nor the richest

The prize goes to every human being willing and
diligent
Refusing discouragement, rising above setbacks
Dismissing ridicule, overcoming obstacles
In order to complete the race.
It is a race to the finish
Not based on education, finances or social status;
A race to unveil purpose, achieve goals, fulfill
destiny
It's the human race!
Today, a challenge has been placed before you.
To stop standing on the sidelines applauding others
Even cheerleaders must run in this race
So I say to thine own self be true...
If you have been drifting on the peripheries of life
Get back in the race!
Get back in the race!
Get back in the race!
It's the human race...

"For
I know the plans
I have for you,"
declares the
LORD, "plans to
prosper you and not to
harm you, plans to
give you
hope and a future."
Jeremiah 29:11 NIV

A Woman of Hope

We are sisters, daughters
Mothers and wives.
Many roles to fulfill during the
Course of our lives.

Our journey has seasons
Of frustration and tears.
Disappointments are many
Down through the years.

Once Christ is allowed
To rule in our hearts,
New courage and strength
He begins to impart.

Life can be cruel
Sometimes it's difficult to cope
Let Jesus make you
A woman of hope.

I
alone am
God!
There are no other
gods;
NO ONE
is like me.
Isaiah 46:9 NCV

YOU *Alone…*

It was YOU…
Who loved me
Like no one else could,
Who believed in me
When no one else would,
Who saved my soul
By shedding Your own precious blood.
It was *YOU*, and *YOU* alone…

It was *YOU*…
Who sustained me
Throughout the years,
Who gave me strength
To face and conquer all my fears,
Who ever so gently
Wiped away every tear.
It was *YOU*, and *YOU* alone…

It was *YOU*…
Who bore my grief
You freed me from a life of shame.
Since our first encounter,
Life for me has never been the same,

That's the reason why
I shall forever praise your Holy name
For it was *YOU*, and *YOU* alone…

`110

Are you a Poet?

And don't know it?
Let's see...
Try these poetry
Prompts...

Sight

Take a moment to admire the sky and its element. What thoughts fill your mind? What wonder fills your heart?
Describe it in a poem...remember poem does not have to rhyme...

_____

_____

_____

_____

_____

_____

_____

_____

_____

_____

_____

_____

_____

_____

_____

Sound

Choose a place. Close your eyes. What sounds do you hear?
Write a poem to describe them...

_____

_____

_____

_____

_____

_____

_____

_____

_____

_____

_____

_____

_____

_____

Taste

What's your favorite food? Describe how it taste and how you feel while eating it.

_____

_____

_____

_____

_____

_____

_____

_____

_____

_____

_____

_____

_____

_____

Touch

Have you ever felt the presence of the Lord? If so, write a poem to describe how it felt. If not, Write a poem telling Him that you desire to feel His presence...

_____

_____

_____

_____

_____

_____

_____

_____

_____

_____

_____

_____

_____

_____

_____

_____

Therefore
if any man be in
Christ,

he is a new creature:
old things are passed
away; behold, all
things are become new.

2 Corinthians 5:17 KJV

The Change

Surrendering

My life to Christ

Set change in motion

Imperceptible at first

While following Him

My life illuminated

With new possibilities

Old things soon shredded

New things embraced

Then all the world

Beheld

The change.

Prayer

Do you find yourself feeling frustrated or in despair with the circumstances of your life? If you have never experienced Jesus as your personal Savior—You too, can experience "The Change." If you wandered off the path and feelings of unworthiness hold you hostage and prevent you from reaching out to God, who so loves you—You too can experience "The Change." Pray this prayer.

Jesus, I am ready for change. Living life on my own terms has not worked. I believe that you are the Son of God and that you died for my sins. I need you. And TODAY, I repent of my sins, I receive you as my Personal Savior. I want to experience the change that I have heard so many others talking about. Today I pray that you will teach me your word and show me your ways.
In Jesus Name

Amen

About the Author

Jeri dropped out of high school in the twelfth grade during mid-term examinations. At age seventeen she survived a suicide attempt and wandered through life feeling hopeless. Physical, emotional and sexual abuse are some of the challenges that severely damaged her self-esteem. "Why am I here!" She often demanded a reply from the Creator while trying to justify a purpose for her existence.

Without vision, plan, direction or purpose for her life she was rescued by an unexpected encounter by the Living God. Jeri is certain that satan plans for her included death, imprisonment or a mental institution. Instead God ordered her steps which led to earning a college degree and a career in nursing. Instead of being treated for mental illness; God raised her up to serve in the mental health field for over twenty-five years bringing light, comfort and encouragement to many others.

Jeri has ministered in the county jail, local prison, halfway houses and homeless shelters. She has spoken at conferences, single's ministry and churches. Jeri host a weekly Facebook Vlog titled "Seasoned for *THIS* Season!" Her live recordings are a source of encouragement and inspiration to God's seasoned people who for various reasons may be sitting on the sidelines of life.

Jeri has over a hundred publishing credits in various magazines including Decision Magazine. Her work has been featured in several anthologies including "Chicken Soup for the Nurses Soul, a Second Dose."

Jeri is the single mother of four children. She has published two devotionals for singles titled,

"Stepping Stones, Reflections for Singles" and Seasoned for this "Season, Reflections for Seasoned Singles." Jeri Darby is an Author, Speaker and Writing Coach who believes that everything in life is a steppingstone. She uses the steppingstones in her life to soar into her destiny while helping others along the way.

If you are seeking a speaker for your event you can contact Jeri Darby:
989 717-1031
araritypress@gmail.com
FB: Jeri Darby
FB: Jeri Darby Speaks

Watch for these Titles
Scheduled for Release

2019

By
Jeri Darby!

"I *AM* a Writer!"
Are you an aspiring author?
Do you battle inner voices that leave you feeling
defeated before you even get started?

If you answered "YES!" to any of these...
Then this book is for you!

"Say So!"
Everyone knows the importance of declaring the
word of God over their lives—*right!*
Well, maybe not everyone...but even though many
know it's a divine strategy for victory sometimes our
mouth just doesn't want to cooperate.
This book will offer a fresh look at the power of
Saying So!

More Titles

By

Jeri Darby

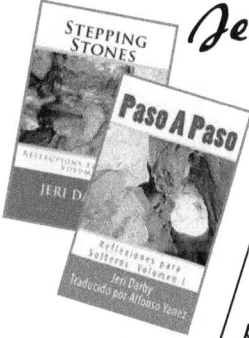

Jeri's first book, "Stepping Stones, Reflections for Single's" is also available in Spanish. It is written in devotional style and is a great resource for those who are recently divorced or prayerfully considering entering the covenant of marriage. $11.99

Seasoned for this Season! Reflections for Seasoned Single's is the second devotional written by Jeri Darby.

This resource if great for those in their seasoned years, those who have lost a spouse and those who have been single for a Lo---nnng Time. $15

Both great for your Single's Discussion Groups!

Order your autographed copies at link below:
https://squareup.com/store/ararity-press
Also available on Amazon!

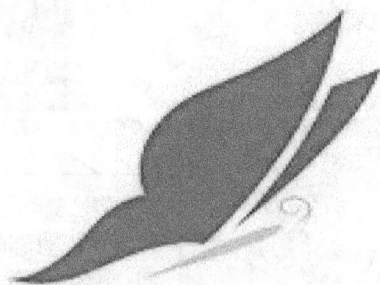

Stepping Stones
Soar into Your Destiny!

www.ingramcontent.com/pod-product-compliance
Lightning Source LLC
LaVergne TN
LVHW021350080426
835508LV00020B/2217